# she is a wolf

Leya Noir

CONTENTS

There are no chapters. There are only things that haunt me,
and things that have set me free. Please proceed with caution, and enjoy.

These poems do not live: it's a sad diagnosis.
They grew their toes and fingers well enough,
Their little foreheads bulged with concentration.
If they missed out on walking about like people
It wasn't for any lack of mother-love.


-Sylvia Plath, 1960

I have conquered the ocean and the sky
but I have yet to conquer you,
or my fear of absolutely everything

My dreams have grown
a mind of their own
so even though I've erased your face
from my thoughts,
it creeps in no matter how much
I pray that it not

I keep lying to strangers
telling them I'm alright
when I'm not
They're the only ones who believe me

When you grow up in a haunted house
where your best friends
are the monsters under your bed,
not much else can scare you.
…except you… I wasn't ready for the devil.

There is no method to my madness
or an answer as to why
I just cannot say no to you
no matter how hard I try

He loves his little monster
and the way I do my hair
He knows I'm fucking wild
and he hates to have me shared
His words crawl up my legs
in the middle of the night
And even though I sleep alone
I can always feel his bite

There used to be a gold chain on my door
separating me from you
You broke my heart
And then you broke that gold chain, too

All of these words that I regurgitate
must've come from something that I once ate
Love, lies, and memories
But mostly, from hate

She has thick skin
and thin patience
and a wavering willpower
for men who push her
just a little too far

You really did know
how to make me smile
I was careful then,
you were fucking wild
I didn't know I was dead
until you brought me to life
I had my pen,
you had your knife
I wrote you down,
but didn't realize
a stab wound came
with each of your lies
and now all I do
is simply fantasize
about that bullet I should have put
between your eyes
Now each breath you take
you can thank me for
I should have shot you the night
you broke down my door

Mirrors hurt more
than they ever have before
To have to look into the eyes of your own evil
leaves your mind at complete war

Sleep seems to elude me
just like your presence
or the pressure of your arms across my stomach
I keep quiet in my bed
let your voice play in my head
and pretend that the nightmare is over
but the nightmare doesn't cease
so I'm praying for my peace
and hoping, some day, this will all feel right
So I button my buttons
and zip my zippers,
trying to fill up my days and keep a routine
But still the shame shows on my face
because there's no ending to this race
No end in sight to hold onto late at night

We spent two years in that tiny apartment,
broke, and drunk only on our love
But that love wasn't able to transcend
into anything real
because back then,
I was a dreamer and a fool
and not much has changed
I'm beginning to wonder if I'll ever be real,
or take the time to ever get to really know
anyone at all

He said he always wondered how a girl like me
could still be
all alone
Maybe it's because I have a fire raging inside
and a desire not to be kept in a cage
He meant for it to hurt my feelings
but it ultimately set me free

How do you mourn something that is still alive?
I kiss your red lips and breathe you in,
regretting every minute from here on out
that I won't spend with you
I'm mourning a life that hasn't yet died

As I quietly
drink my quiet tea
I press my palms over my ears
and wish for you to be quiet
You are so beautiful
when you aren't lying

I want to walk this world alone
until I'm weathered down to bone
and in that process if I meet
a man to sweep me off my feet…
He'll have to set my heart ablaze
with flames so hot, they burn my face
He'll have to set my life on fire
never bore me, never tire
He can't go sing to other girls
with longer legs and tighter curls
I'll have to be the only one
that he can covet like the sun
But if it seems that there are more
and loving him becomes a chore
then I will leave, I'll run away
I'd rather be alone than stay

Let's bathe in each others wickedness
until we emerge
unrecognizable to the other person

I have not yet decided
whether to love you or kill you
But I can assure you,
when I decide, you'll be the first to know

And then, there was a defining moment
that I remember
I stopped wanting to be with you
and I just wanted to become you
Evil, cunning, not giving a fuck
and now we can drink until the sun comes up
until all of the bottles are empty
and our lips can spill over each other
and onto other people's lips
…And none of it even matters

I don't know why I put myself through it,
the way that I do.


For you.

I wonder what new scars you've accrued
while I was in the dark
playing in the nude
Me, well I've burnt my wrist
cut open my finger
On our old street,
I lurk and I linger
I stalk you at night
I creep in the day
I get caught when you sleep
Right before you pray
You're praying for me
I know it
I can feel it
You wonder if I'm all alone
You need it
You breathe it

I carry the weight of your heart
but it's all for show
You don't actually have one

People forget that there were those
in our lives before them,
and others even before those.
Sometimes they matter,
And sometimes, they don't.

Once upon a time
there was a man who made me laugh
He took my breath away
but I knew it wouldn't last
he grew tired of my voice
and the way I held my pain
He slept with other girls
when he had nothing more to gain
And so I crumble every night
when I am all alone
But I still carry my smile
and it remains unknown

He called me a savage and I rolled my eyes
then I threw up my arms, crossed my legs at my thighs
If I'm such a savage what does that make you?
I don't understand what you're trying to do
If I'm such a savage then why do you stay?
The way that we argue isn't okay
If I'm such a savage then how will this end?
Lonely and broken? My heart on the mend?
If I'm such a savage then let's cut our ties
I've gotten too good at rolling my eyes

I'm sorry I don't have the right words for you
or even enough of them
I used them all up
screaming in my dreams
and bargaining with the devil

And it looks like I have everything from far away
but since you've been gone, all I have is today
My throne is empty, my love is at bay
You left me with my pride, and nothing more to say

He said "I think there's blood on your stairs"
I said "You might be right"
Men have tried to climb up them
to keep me warm at night
Many have tried, few have made it,
even less have succeeded
They cut their heels to get to me
past warnings they never heeded
You think that you're the only one
who is trying to be the only one?
While you are out with other girls
you think that I'm the lonely one
But you are wrong, I'm as bad as you
I'm just sly and I never get caught
I know every sin you've ever committed,
every drink for someone else you've bought

I feel you
In my broken doors
In my empty bed
You might not realize that
the things you do leave scars

I will forever have an open bottle of wine
on my nightstand
My glasses, papers, and pens strewn across my bed
And an empty space next to me
that you used to call yours

Reading through your writings
you're more cruel than you appear
I knew you as sweet but negligent
I felt ignored for years
For while you were fast asleep,
I ate breakfast and lived my life
And though you always showed up for me
you never made me your wife
And now we're way past broken
It's been one of my worst fears
So I'll always hold you dearly
through the rest of all my years
(However long they may be
but you can no longer taste my tears)

Not many people know how many songs
and poems have been written about me,
but me
I collect them and look back when I need a reminder
of how vicious these claws can be
Too many of you know where I live
and too many of you don't respect it
You crawl through my locked doors
without invitation
and my trust and my body is expected
And although you and I are no longer connected,
I'm still naked in my bed
everything is just how you left it

He is my rock
but he is also my anchor
pulling me down, down
making me drown, drown

She has a man who only half loves her
but makes her feel alive
While the other man is pushed aside,
for her, he only has eyes
And though all she'll ever be is a pretty little fool
she carries the weight of both hearts on her shoulders,
they feel like boulders and wool

We bit our filters off
so our snake tongues
now hiss at each other,
never showing mercy

And that's why I'd rather have my horns on display
for everyone to see
so they can see what they're getting into
when they get into it with me
Everyone knows that I'd rather have a pair
of hands around my throat
than have a fake halo slip off my head
and make me choke

You use your love as a weapon
taking it away as you see fit
and putting it back when it's convenient

They say distance makes the hearts grow fonder
but I know it only makes your eyes wander

To be honest, hanging out in the gutter
with you was a blast
and I wouldn't change it because now it's my past
The lessons that I got from it will continue to last
I'll remember that winter, and the boy who lived
in the trash

What you heard was true
I do avoid the light
so I can make more space at night
for the ones who like to call me theirs
All of my bones and all of my hairs

I remember the way the night
cast shadows on your face
and the way you looked in my
rearview mirror as I drove away

How do you expect to make
a genuine connection with me
when you're connecting with everyone else?
The only difference between insanity and sanity
is perspective
and you, my dear, are a little outside of the lines
and I've taken you outside of my mind

The difference between predators
and scavengers
is obvious
He ate my flesh
while you just picked
on my bones

You may have come out of the dark
with wings stapled to your back,
but you are no devil,
simply a man who is good at arts and crafts

I was born with a broken heart
and a deep desire to find out why

Since I found out you worship ghosts
but disregard the living
then baby, R.I.P. to me
the past isn't worth forgiving

I'm tired of turning down
the many lives I should've been living
I'm tired of waiting for the moon
to come out to feel complete
But mostly, I'm tired of sharpening my claws
only to sink my teeth into dinner
that is already dead

I don't wish death upon you
But I dress for your funeral every morning,
just in case

If I'm a bird without a cage
and you're a wolf with thirst and rage
then how on earth did we end up
not being able to turn this page?

My 'ride or dies' are all dead
and now I'm stuck alone in my own head
which is the scariest place I could ever be

This loss I feel is fucking real
I'm empty to my bones
I'll never be anyone if I'm no one to you
no matter how well I'm known

When midnight starts creeping up
so quietly, so sly
I know that you'll find your way into my thoughts
So I turn on every light
and make as much noise
as I possibly can

she is a wolf

One of these days, I'll stop
whispering in my sleep
and summoning devils out of thin air

He hid behind shadows and lies
between other girl's thighs
and pretended to still have a soul

she is a wolf

Stop looking out the window
I know there are better options out there
but I'm right here

Just remember who was there for you
back when all you had to offer was
a beautiful crooked smile
and minimal effort

My love is like a crocodile's jaw
Suffocating, heavy, deadly

I need to get out of this town
the one that makes me suffocate and drown
Because all I see are ugly monsters
plastic faces, seeking sponsors
2 am, makeup wearing thin
desperation setting in
I'd rather set this city on fire
than ever meet another liar

He broke me into pieces
I didn't even know I had

All I hear are devils
And all I see is you
And I'm having a hard time
differentiating between sound and sight

Last night I ate my dinner
off of the tile floor
and drew checkmarks up on my wall
marking the days since we've spoken
I still can't get through to you
All I hear on your side of the phone
is the loud, empty dial tone

I keep thinking that I can make this right
but every night that we meet
under that moon where we found each other,
it only ends in disaster
We can no longer see ourselves in one another

Go home tonight and try to sleep
and try not to think of me
because in the morning when you wake
I won't be who I used to be
And in the morning when you drive to work
please forget to whisper my name
since I'll be fast asleep in dreams
wishing you weren't so ashamed
And when you want to pick up your phone
to call me and hear my voice
I'll be long gone away from this town
You haven't left me much of a choice
I'll sing the songs that you once sang to me
real quiet and almost pretend
and hang my heart out the window to dry,
heal, repair, and mend

He gave me a box and told me
"What's inside is haunted, just like you"
He knows I've died a thousand times
and each time I come back to life
I bring ghosts back with me

I can see the light
dimming in your eyes
and I know this isn't
exactly the right time
but just lie to me
and tell me we'll be fine

And in the end,
the hate subsided
but so did the love
And my heart became so diluted that
it barely even kept me alive

We sang our songs
danced like we were free
I was happy to have your company
but my voice got tired
and your ears got weak
and now we no longer even speak
We started this
making my rules bend
but now you're on the other side of my pen
close the curtains
draw the shades
cut the lights
turn on the rage

Are we saving daylight?
Or is it saving us?
Because I've been gone for days
in my own eternal lust
What do we need to save
if we're not saving time?
I just need to accept the fact
that you're no longer mine

I painted you a backdrop
on your stage tonight
but it all turned out red
Now, there is a small outline
of a girl you used to know
She once stood here
Sometimes she cries
and sometimes she waits for you
to turn around
The red girl with her hopes so high
will die before your eyes

My greatest poetry
comes from conversations with you

If you push hard enough
on the middle of my chest
my ribs will open up
and reveal that my next breath
is for you
and the next, and the next, until death

I handpicked this day for you, my love
The smell of rain in the air
The way the wind blows through my hair
And the calm, quiet creep into the night
To the end
You'll never even see it coming

I chew flesh off bones
it's a very distinct bite
It will leave you reaching out for me
in the middle of the night

You fell for a wolf
but now you're asking why
your back has scratches and gashes
and why I howl at the sky?
My dear boy,
please don't you cry
I'll still need you and feed you
and never leave you to die

Walking through those breezy halls
where that beautiful linen lined the walls
like ghosts
No matter how much I hate you
I'll always be in love
with that one memory

All of our hotel rooms
and rendezvous
Every time you unzipped my dresses
I wore for you
quietly, but so fiercely
You are still my favorite
and best kept secret

I always used to dream about the day
that I'd start to love my nightmares
and now I'm living proof
that dreams do come true

Dear man on the moon,
Tell me, what am I to do?
I've lost lovers and friends
all I see are dead ends
and all I feel
is empty
and excited

I drive home every night
under these city lights
blow kisses at the moon
and I thank the stars
that I no longer drive home
with you

We all need to go crazy for a little while...
or forever

Maybe we needed all of those days away
Maybe all those days away taught us how to stay

It's about damn time I start acting my age
but I'll never stop howling at the moon

Some hearts work
while others don't
Some will love you
when others won't

Through my rusty cage
is where I first came alive
I gave up everything
in order to make that door open

she is a wolf

In my cup of tea
there are storms and wars
for the morning is when my dreams
become distant, fading memories

I fall in love with devils daily
and stay in love until I'm crazy

I'm sorry darling,
but are you complaining about the bites?
You let a wolf in your bed,
what did you expect to happen that night?

I rebuilt my life this year
brick by brick
and I realized if my foundation hadn't crumbled
I'd never be standing at the top
Sometimes you just have to kill and resurrect
in order to get it correct

What you consider to be your worst behavior
is probably me at my best
I crawl and sprawl against the night,
waiting to be undressed
The days are long and the nights are hard,
I'm a damsel in distress
So I'll throw down my hair for you
to give you full access
You know as well as I do
that wild things cannot be caged
and I keep asking them to leave
but the demons stay
until they're saged
The worst part of all of this
is knowing that I'll never change
And I know that you want to leave,
and that can be arranged

All I found on my search
for the real you
was the bottom of many bottles
and I don't think I want to find you
all that much anymore

There are times that I still curl up
into a ball and scream
thank you
at the sky
for getting you far away from me
For surviving

They told me not to forget who I was
but I had to learn the hard way
when I chose destroying myself
as a priority
But now that I'm breathing and eating again,
I can finally see what I missed out on

We can be different people
from day to day
but hopefully we stay
the people we turn into
when everything else
has broken us
into a million different pieces

You satiate my late night appetite
with your howls and your growls
your tongue and your jowls
When my claws come out
and you bare your teeth
under pale moonlight
is where we always meet
until we're exhausted and spent
broken and bent
Then we go back to our packs
and silently wait for our next attack

I'll be writing about that night
for a very long time to come
You traced your fingers over the shape
of my body just for fun

There is a certain freedom to living this way
No one in your path, no promises to stay
Sticking knives in everyone you meet
Climbing to hell while accepting defeat
Splinters in your eyes so you can't even see
all the madness inside that rages in me

Although my lips
look like heaven
that doesn't mean you should trust me
any more than I give you a reason to

I want to tug on your hair
in the shower
lying around
not minding the hours
voicing our dreams
planning our days
no longer stuck
in our resentful ways
pointing to a map
driving to the sea
living in love
that's so foreign to me

He told me that I'm beautiful
and that I'm down to earth
I laughed and said
"well baby, it's because I know my worth"

I behave so badly
under the sheets
every time we meet
And I'm not any better
in the street
when you take me out to eat
I stay on my worst behavior
but you still call me sweet

When I stopped being afraid of the dark
I found my monsters
and started playing with them

When I was with you
I felt so alive
like I've never felt
in my entire life
Unfortunately,
I'm still chasing that high
And even though
I wish you'd die
at least you're killing someone
else's dreams
and no longer mine

Some people don't remember their dreams
My problem is that I only remember my dreams
and none of the other important things

She said you won't be going to hell
but that means she doesn't know you that well
Because hell is where I'll be
and everyone knows that
you can't stand to be away from me

People are always wondering how I write
I just take the contents out of my life
I'll gaze at some art or a map or a book
or someone who wouldn't usually
get a second look
I chew them all up to see how they taste
then I spit them all out and I start to create
Most don't think there's much going on
underneath my black hair
but I assure you, there's so much more
beyond my blank stare
In between my eyes are all my lovers that I've killed
I slit all their throats
drank their blood that I've spilled
Yet, I awake them from the dead when they need to
inspire
I made them immortal, so they dare not tire
When I am done, I put them back to sleep
and wonder what else in this world I could possibly eat

Any friend who has ever said
"you're on your own"
is no friend of mine

Maybe we need to be broken
so we can appreciate how whole we once were
and how beautiful and patient the art of fixing
something is


    ... we need less trash cans and more recycling bins

I never even saw you coming
and I never would have guessed
that your eyes would catch me so off guard
and turn my world upside down

My broken heart
can't tell what's true
but these broken hands
can still love you

She picked wildflowers
and drank whiskey
and ran as far away from anything
that could render her obedient

Just because you treated me better
than you've ever treated anyone else
doesn't mean that's the best
I've ever been treated

It's incredible how some people
can singlehandedly tear your life apart
and leave only the bones,
while others can help you
back onto your feet
and paste the pieces back together
even better than they were before

I want you to kiss me
but I don't know how to ask
so instead, for now,
I'll just kiss this flask

I'm just the same little old me
Some integral parts have been
chipped away or fallen off,
yet these lungs still contract
and my heart still beats,
only a little off key

I send my grace to you
every single day
for awakening this monster in me
For before,
I was only an empty vessel

and then, one day
it just stops hurting...
you climb out of the ground,
kick over your tombstone,
and excavate your soul

He and I were on a deadline
You and I have nothing but time

I wish I could eat you up without it killing you
I don't want you to die…
I only want our secrets to come to life

Home is where I've always run from
and where I'm running to
But I'm in luck, for all I feel
is at home when I'm with you

whisper in my ear
pull my hair
touch me gently
grab me everywhere

He keeps begging for my heart to beat for him
and my heart keeps telling him "no"

These claws aren't just for show, my dear

I sharpened up my teeth again
since you're no longer here
I bit chunks from my lips today
since I disappeared
My words are sharp, my temper's hot
My claws are freshly filed
I'm no longer red riding hood,
that fairy tale's tired
I'm the new hero, I'm the wolf
that you hear howling in your dreams
and I don't need a savior
I just need to hear your screams

Okay
So I'm friendly, elusive, obscure
However, did you ever consider why, sir?
We could sit around the table,
drink whiskey all night
You'd still leave me trembling, questioning why
Why am I broken? So insecure?
You have no idea what I have endured
But you hold me for hours, talk to me despite
the way I get drunk and fight every night

Sometimes, even the most evil of people
can change for the right person
Even the devil must have a weakness


Sometimes, you are just someone's 'something'.

He told me that
my hate turns him on
...so I decided to hate him
all night long

Your clothes and your scent
now clutter up my room
and it's strange I let you in
since I consider this my tomb
But here you are,
alive and breathing
Red velvet cheeks,
heart pounding while beating
And I can't decide if I will
devour you or not
so let's just roll around
and pray we don't get caught

When we're all alone is when we realize
who we really are
and who we've grown to be
And I think my heart gets a little warmed over
when you're alone with me

I light matches
to cut into the darkness
as the darkness
has cut into me

All these comings and goings,
all these mysteries and knowing's,
and all I truly care about
is following you wherever you might wander

He brings me flowers
and says he's proud of me
and maybe that's all I'll ever really need

We have all these moments
that we have to fill up
And I just hope that
I get to fill them up with you

Stars are falling to the left and right of me
Whispering "look up, baby, pay attention, can't you
see?"
They're all dying just to make me happy

I've turned men into monsters
I've mistaken a peasant for a king
My life is made up of dangerous things

I leave rose petals
wherever I go
like breadcrumbs
in case you ever want to
find me again

He said that he likes imperfections
and I know that's why he likes me

I hang out in the lost and found
knowing you'll find me
when you come back around

I know you all think that I put
all of my secrets on display
On the contrary, I actually
keep them all locked away
Most people look at me
and see the brightness of day
But in fact, I'm responsible
for a lot of death and decay

I caught a dragonfly today
and I tied up his tail with some string
and then I flew him like a kite
I treated him like a thing
But he was not mine to keep
So I untied his tail
Kissed his little wings goodbye
And I wished him
Farewell

How quick we are to ignore
not only the red flags,
but the mountains that they are planted in

The worst thing in the world
is letting someone know
that they are about to lose you,
and them being alright with it

I have yet to be satiated,
but I'm saving all my hunger
for you

Sometimes,
I have to keep my eyes open
when I'm told to keep them shut
I need to see what other people won't

I could make you a map
to my heart
but I know
you'd still get lost

I wish to have your eyes
forever sewn to mine
while towards your lips I climb
past the burning pages
and through the unlocked door
with my lifeless hand in yours
we'll be kissing on the floor
Words are written and rewritten
my heart is yours to keep
I kiss you goodnight, every night
in my deepest sleep

I feel my pulse
in my fingers
and in this pen
stronger than in my
heart or head

We're
all
recovering
from
someone

and if we die tonight,
please bury us in the stars
it will be you, me,
and everything we were supposed to be

Loving you
was the smartest thing
I ever chose to do

I used to stitch my heart
into the pockets of your clothes
and each night you'd find my
hidden heart,
and rip it out

The lining of my stomach
has become weak
from excessive alcohol
and thoughts of you

I don't trust you
because I don't trust myself
or anybody else

I'll never tire
of not having to piece together
my nights
based on flashbacks
and empty cans and bottles
anymore

Leya Noir

I want to crack your skull open
to see what makes you tick
and to see
how I can make it me

Give me a reason
to wear my new dress
with slits so high
they'll burn your eyes
Give me a reason
to take my next breath
and I'll never again
let you hang out to dry

Why do I still dream about you
when you were such a nightmare?
It's unfortunate I think about you
every time I touch my hair
for there are missing pieces
and I need to let them grow
There are pieces of you still in me
and I hate to let them show
So I lock up all my broken doors,
the ones you broke in spite
and I cling to the moon and the stars
praying to make it through the night

Of all the goodbyes I said this year
yours was the worst I had to hear
because when I said goodbye to you
it left me choking, dead and blue
We'll never say hello again
so I'll talk to you through my black pen
And when you read what I have to say
you can close the book, or just turn the page

you are the most beautiful monster
that I have ever met
I don't know what part of my soul died
to let you seep into my veins
but it's way past midnight
and this is the time where nothing good ever happens
I started to trade sleep for your poisonous kisses
and now I'm so full and sick  of them,
I want you gone
Goodbye, savage
it's time to wash my face and put my clothes back on
and live like I've never lost someone like you

she is a wolf

## ABOUT THE WOLF

I was mad. I was so fucking mad. didn't he know who I was? didn't he know who he tried to destroy? but that's the thing about us wolves, we are not only resilient survivors, we are fighters. thank you for carrying this piece of me with you. if you are reading this, you are now and forever a part of my pack.

Made in the USA
Middletown, DE
24 April 2018